The Most Amazing Story

SECOND EDITION

Workbook

The Most Amazing Story-Workbook

By Wanda Nazworth

The Most Amazing Story

SECOND EDITION

Workbook

Distributed by Wanda Nazworth and DM2 International Inc.

Disciple Makers Multiplied
PO Box 3570
Harlingen, TX 78551
For more information:
Email: wnazworth@gmail.com
www.DM2USA.org

Copyright

Scripture passages quoted are from the New King James Version, 1997, Thomas Nelson, Inc.

Coloring pages by Jim LeGette

The Most Amazing Story-Workbook

Lesson 1—**The Most Wonderful Letter**

Memory Verse

> *All Scripture is given by inspiration of God [....] 2 Timothy 3:16a*

Questions

1. To whom did God write His letter, the Bible? _____
   _____

2. What was God's reason for writing us a letter? _____
   _____
   _____

3. What were the men called who wrote God's words in the Bible? _____
   _____

4. How many prophets did God use to write His letter? _____
   _____

5. Did the prophets write exactly what God wanted them to write, or did they add some
   of their own ideas? _____
   _____

6. How long did it take for the entire Bible to be written? _____
   _____

7. How can the whole Bible agree when it was written by so many different men? ____
   _____

8. Is every part of the Bible true? _____
   _____

9. The Bible is divided into two parts. What are these two parts called? _____
   _____

10. Does the Bible say the same thing today as what the prophets wrote in the scrolls
    long ago? _____
    _____
    _____

(Answers in *The Most Amazing Story*, pages 19-20)

Lesson 2—**Who is God?**

Memory Verse

Before the mountains were brought forth, or ever You had formed the earth and the world, even from everlasting to everlasting, You are God. Psalm 90:2

Questions

1. When did God come into being? _____
   _____

2. Will God ever die? _____
   _____

3. What are some things you need in order to stay alive? _____
   _____

4. What does God need in order to stay alive? _____
   _____
   _____

5. Does God have a body like you and I do? _____
   _____
   _____

6. Is God a real person, or is He simply a force? _____
   _____
   _____

7. Why is it impossible to hide from God? _____
   _____

8. How can you get to know God? _____
   _____
   _____

9. How many Gods are there? _____
   _____

10. Who is in charge of the whole world? _____
    _____
    _____

(Answers in *The Most Amazing Story*, page 26)

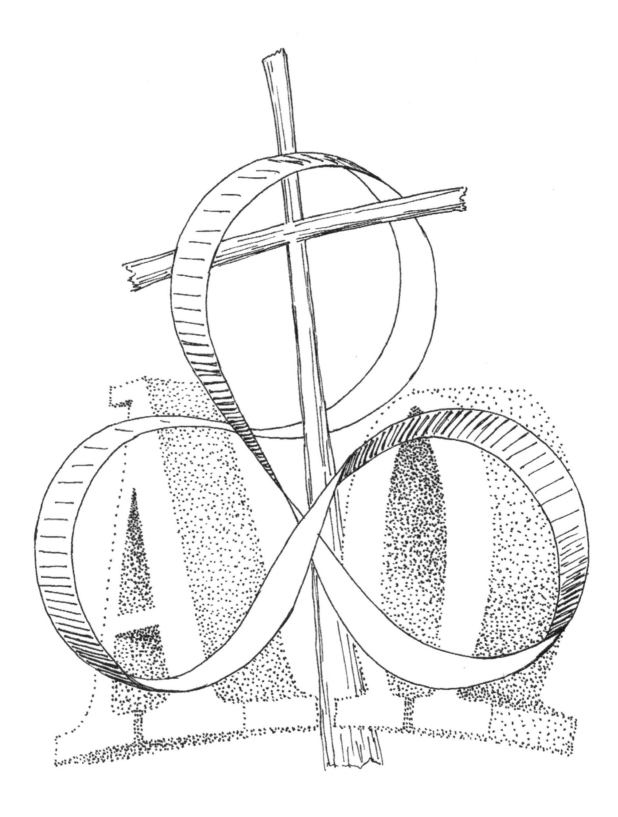

Lesson 3—**In the Beginning**

Memory Verse

> *Before the mountains were brought forth, or ever You had formed the earth and the world, even from everlasting to everlasting, You are God. Psalm 90:2*

Questions

1. Why is God the only One who can tell us how everything came into being in the beginning? _____
   _____
   _____
   _____

2. What was the earth like in the beginning? _____
   _____
   _____

3. In the darkness, who was hovering over the water? _____
   _____
   _____

4. How was it possible for God to make the light shine just by speaking? _____
   _____
   _____

5. Who taught God how to make light? _____
   _____

6. What did God do on the second day? _____
   _____
   _____

7. On the third day, what did God make? _____
   _____

8. When God looked at His work, was He happy with all He had made? _____
   _____
   _____
   _____

(Answers in *The Most Amazing Story*, page 32)

Lesson 4—**A Wonderful World**

Memory Verse

Ah, Lord GOD! Behold, You have made the heavens and the earth by Your great power and outstretched arm. There is nothing too hard for You. Jeremiah 32:17

Questions

1. How did God create the plants and animals? _____
    _____
    _____

2. What did God give to plants so they could produce more plants just like themselves?
    _____
    _____

3. How did God know how to make the sun, moon, stars, and all the plants and animals? _____
    _____
    _____

4. Why did God make so many different kinds of plants and animals? Why did He make so many lovely colors, smells, and tastes? _____
    _____
    _____
    _____

5. What did God put in the sky on the fourth day so that we could keep track of days, months, and years? _____
    _____

6. Can you hide from God? _____
    _____
    _____

7. Was there anything wrong with any part of the world God made? _____
    _____
    _____
    _____

(Answers in *The Most Amazing Story*, page 38)

Lesson 5—**Mission Completed**

Memory Verse

Ah, Lord GOD! Behold, You have made the heavens and the earth by Your great power and outstretched arm. There is nothing too hard for You. Jeremiah 32:17

Questions

1. For whom did God make the world and everything in it? _____
_____
_____

2. Name some ways God made people to be like Him? _____
_____
_____
_____

3. Who is the only One who can give life? _____
_____
_____

4. When God starts to do something, does He always finish it? _____
_____
_____

5. Does God sometimes mess up on a project? _____
_____
_____

6. Was God exhausted when He finished creating the world and everything in it? ____
_____

7. What was so special about the seventh day of the week? _____
_____
_____
_____

8. Why is God the One in charge of the world? _____
_____
_____
_____

(Answers in *The Most Amazing Story*, page 44)

Lesson 6—**Special Helpers**

Memory Verse

For by Him all things were created that are in heaven and that are on earth, visible and invisible [...] All things were created through Him and for Him. Colossians 1:16

Questions

1. Is God greater than the angels? _____
   _____

2. When God made the angels, what did He want the angels to do? _____
   _____
   _____

3. Why was it okay for God to tell the angels what to do? _____
   _____
   _____

4. Did God force the angels to follow Him? _____
   _____

5. Do angels have bodies like you and I do? _____
   _____

6. Can angels be everywhere at the same time? _____
   _____

7. Are angels strong and smart? _____
   _____
   _____
   _____

8. When God first made the angels, was there any part of them that was bad? _____
   _____

9. How could God make so many angels? _____
   _____

10. Where did the angels live when God first made them? _____
    _____
    _____

(Answers in *The Most Amazing Story*, page 50)

Lesson 7—**The Rebel Angel**

Memory Verse

A haughty look, a proud heart [...] are sin. Proverbs 21:4

Questions

1. What does the name Lucifer mean? _____
   _____

2. Who made Lucifer beautiful and wise? _____
   _____

3. Was there anything bad about Lucifer when God created him? _ _____
   _____

4. What wrong thoughts did Lucifer begin to have? _____
   _____
   _____

5. Could Lucifer and all his followers overthrow God? _____
   _____
   _____

6. Can anyone who is evil live with God in Heaven? _____
   _____
   _____

7. What does the name Satan mean? _____
   _____

8. What does the name devil mean? _____
   _____

9. What are Satan and his demons doing right now? _____
   _____

10. What will happen to Satan and his demons someday? _____
    _____
    _____
    _____

(Answers in *The Most Amazing Story*, pages 55-56)

Lesson 8—**The First Parents**

Memory Verse

The earth is the Lord's, and all its fullness, the world and those who dwell therein. Psalm 24:1

Questions

1. Was it right for God to put Adam in the garden and give him a job without asking him first? _____
    _____
    _____
    _____

2. Did God know what Adam needed? _____
    _____
    _____
    _____

3. Who was the only One who could provide a wife for Adam? _____
    _____

4. Was anything wrong with the things God provided for Adam? _____
    _____
    _____
    _____

5. Why were Adam and Eve not embarrassed when they were naked? _____
    _____

6. Why did God make both a man and a woman? _____
    _____

7. What was God's plan for Adam and Eve and their children? _____
    _____

8. Did God tell Adam and Eve what He wanted them to do, or did God just leave them to guess about what He wanted? _____
    _____

9. Who do all people in the world come from? _____
    _____

(Answers in *The Most Amazing Story*, page 62)

Lesson 9—**Separated**

Memory Verse

The earth is the Lord's, and all its fullness, the world and those who dwell therein. Psalm 24:1

Questions

1. What two special trees did God put in the middle of the garden? _____
    _____
    _____

2. Of all the trees in the garden, from which one tree did God tell Adam and Eve not to eat? _____
    _____

3. Why did God put one forbidden tree in the garden? _____
    _____
    _____
    _____

4. What did God say would happen to Adam and Eve if they ate from The Tree of the Knowledge of Good and Evil? _____
    _____
    _____

5. If Adam and Eve became separated from God, what would happen to their bodies?
    _____

6. What would happen to Adam and Eve's soul and spirit (their real selves) when their bodies died? _____
    _____

7. What did Satan say would happen to Adam and Eve if they ate from The Tree of the Knowledge of Good and Evil? _____
    _____
    _____

8. Who was telling the truth, God or Satan? _____
    _____

9. When Adam and Eve believed Satan instead of God, whose side did they join? _____
    _____

10. After Adam and Eve became separated from God, could they do anything to please God? _____
    _____

11. How can you keep from being tricked by Satan? _____
    _____
    _____
    _____

(Answers in *The Most Amazing Story*, page 68-69)

Lesson 10—**Consequences**

Memory Verse

Therefore, just as through one man sin entered the world, and death through sin, and thus death spread to all men, because all sinned. Romans 5:12

Questions

1. Could Adam and Eve hide from God? _____
_____

2. Why did God have the right to question Adam and Eve about what they had done?
_____
_____

3. Who did God plan to send to rescue people from Satan's dominion?
_____
_____

4. Does God always complete His plans? _____
_____

5. How did God show mercy to Adam and Eve? _____
_____

6. How did God show grace to Adam and Eve? _____
_____

7. What happened to the perfect earth because of what Adam did? _____
_____
_____
_____

8. What is sin? _____

9. What is the penalty for sin? _____
_____

10. Does God know everything you have ever done? _____
_____
_____

(Answers in *The Most Amazing Story*, pages 76-77)

Lesson 11—**Banished**

Memory Verse

> *Therefore, just as through one man sin entered the world, and death through sin, and thus death spread to all men, because all sinned. Romans 5:12*

Questions

1. When Adam and Eve realized they were naked, did they ask God to make clothes for them? _____

   _____

2. Was God pleased with the clothes Adam and Eve made? _____

   _____

3. Who was the only One who could make acceptable clothes for Adam and Eve? ____

   _____

4. How did God make acceptable clothes for Adam and Eve? _____

   _____

5. What is the penalty for doing what God says not to do, or sinning? _____

   _____

6. Why did God not let Adam and Eve eat from The Tree of Life? _____

   _____

7. Was there any way for Adam and Eve to sneak past God's angels and get back into the garden? _____

   _____

8. Who gave life to Cain and Abel?

   _____

9. Into whose family were you born? _____

   _____

10. Is there anything you can do to make yourself acceptable to God so that you can live with Him forever? _____

    _____

(Answers in *The Most Amazing Story*, page 82)

Lesson 12—An Unacceptable Offering

Memory Verse

There is a way that seems right to a man, but its end is the way of death. Proverbs 14:12

Questions

1. Did Cain know how God wanted him to come to Him? _____
    _____
    _____
    _____

2. How did God want Cain and Abel to come to Him to be made acceptable? _____
    _____

3. What did Cain offer to God? _____
    _____

4. Why did Cain not come to God in the way God had shown him to come? _____
    _____
    _____

5. Did God give Cain a chance to change his mind and come to Him in the right way?
    _____
    _____

6. Why is murder wrong? _____
    _____
    _____

7. What happened to Cain's family? _____
    _____
    _____

8. What was the name of the son God gave Eve to replace Abel? _____
    _____
    _____

9. Who is the only One who can save you from Satan and death? _____
    _____
    _____
    _____

(Answers in *The Most Amazing Story*, page 88)

Lesson 13—**Noah**

Memory Verse

> *"For I have no pleasure in the death of one who dies," says the Lord God. "Therefore turn and live!" Ezekiel 18:32*

Questions

1. Why did Adam and Eve's children reject God? _____

2. What were the people like in the days of Noah? _____
_____
_____
_____

3. Was Noah a sinner like everyone else? _____
_____
_____

4. Who was the only One who could save Noah and his family from the flood? _____
_____
_____

5. Why did God save Noah from the flood? _____
_____

6. Why did Noah build the boat exactly like God said? _____
_____
_____
_____

7. Is God happy about people being separated from Him? _____
_____

8. What is the penalty for sin? _____
_____

9. Can you save yourself from this death penalty? _____
_____

10. Who is the only One who can save you from death?_____
_____

11. Who did God say He would send to make a way for you to be saved from Satan, sin, and death? _____
_____
_____

(Answers in *The Most Amazing Story*, page 96)

Lesson 14—**The Terrible Flood**

Memory Verse

I, even I, am the Lord, and besides Me there is no savior. Isaiah 43:11

Questions

1. Does God always do what He promises to do? _____
   _____

2. Is anything too hard for God? _____
   _____

3. How old were Abraham and Sarah when Isaac was born?_____
   _____

4. Why was it okay for God to tell Abraham to sacrifice Isaac? _____
   _____
   _____

5. When God asked Abraham to sacrifice his only son, did Abraham think God had
   changed His mind about giving him many descendants? _____
   _____
   _____
   _____

6. In what way are you like Isaac on the altar? _____
   _____
   _____

7. Who was the only One who could provide a way for Isaac to escape death? _____
   _____

8. What did God provide for Isaac? _____
   _____

9. Who is the only One who can provide a way for you to escape death? _____
   _____

10. Who did God say would come from Abraham's descendants to help all the families
    of the earth? _____
    _____
    _____

(Answers in *The Most Amazing Story*, page 101)

Lesson 15—**God's Promises**

Memory Verse

> *That they may know that You, whose name alone is the Lord, are the Most High over all the earth. Psalm 83:18*

Questions

1. Did God forget about Noah and his family when they were in the boat? _____
   _____
   _____

2. Why could God tell the wind and the water what do? _____
   _____
   _____

3. What did Noah's sacrifice show about his belief in God? _____
   _____
   _____

4. For whom did God make the earth and everything on it? _____
   _____

5. Will God ever destroy the whole earth with a flood again? _____
   _____
   _____

6. After the flood, what did God tell Noah to do? _____
   _____
   _____

7. Did God have the right to put people in charge of the earth? _____
   _____
   _____

8. What does God want us to remember whenever we see a rainbow? _____
   _____
   _____
   _____

(Answers in *The Most Amazing Story*, page 107)

Lesson 16—**Confusion**

Memory Verse

That they may know that You, whose name alone is the Lord, are the Most High over all the earth. Psalm 83:18

Questions

1. What did God tell Noah and his sons to do? _____
    _____

2. Did Noah's descendants spread out all over the earth like God told them to?_____
    _____

3. Did Noah's descendants think they could go against God and get away it? _____
    _____
    _____

4. Did God know that the people were not following His directions? _____
    _____

5. What did God do to make the people fill the earth like He had told them to do? ____
    _____
    _____

6. What happened to Lucifer when he tried to take God's place in Heaven? _____
    _____

7. What happened to Adam and Eve when they believed Satan instead of believing God?
    _____
    _____

8. What happened to the people in Noah's day when they ignored God?_____
    _____

9. Who is in charge of the world? _____
    _____

10. Is there any religion that can keep you from being separated from God forever in the terrible place of suffering? _____
    _____
    _____
    _____

(Answers in *The Most Amazing Story*, pages 113-114)

Lesson 17—**A Great Nation**

Memory Verse

> *Indeed I have spoken it; I will also bring it to pass. I have purposed it; I will also do it.*
> *Isaiah 46:11b*

Questions

1. After God showed His great power at the flood and at the Tower of Babel, did the people begin to worship God? _____ _____

2. Was God still planning to send the Savior, even though people always turned away from Him and acted wickedly? _____ _____ _____

3. What did God tell Abram to do? _____ _____

4. Why was it okay for God to tell Abram what to do? _____ _____

5. Could Abram have chosen not to do what God said? _____ _____

6. What promises did God make to Abram? _____ _____ _____ _____

7. Did Abram believe these promises? _____ _____

8. Can you trust God to keep His promises? _____ _____

9. What were the Canaanites like? _____ _____

10. Was it right for God to give the Canaanites' land to Abram's descendants? _____ _____ _____

(Answers in *The Most Amazing Story*, page 120)

Lesson 18—**Fire from Heaven**

Memory Verse

Indeed I have spoken it; I will also bring it to pass. I have purposed it; I will also do it.
Isaiah 46:11b

Questions

1. Why did Lot decide to move close to the Jordan River? _____
    _____

2. What were the people like who lived near the Jordan River? _____
    _____

3. Who is the highest authority and judge? _____
    _____

4. What does God say must happen to sinners? _____
    _____

5. Why did God rescue Lot? _____
    _____
    _____

6. Why did God turn Lot's wife into a pillar of salt? _____
    _____
    _____

7. What did God do to the cities of Sodom and Gomorrah? _____
    _____
    _____
    _____

8. Was there any way for the people of Sodom and Gomorrah to escape God's
    punishment? _____
    _____

9. Who was the only One who could rescue Lot from death? _____
    _____

10. Who is the only One who can rescue you from the death penalty you deserve for your
    sin? _____
    _____

(Answers in *The Most Amazing Story*, page 127)

Lesson 19—**More than the Stars**

Memory Verse

> *And he believed in the Lord, and He accounted it to him for righteousness.*
> *Genesis 15:6*

Questions

1. After Lot moved away, what did God say He would give to Abraham? _____
    _____
    _____

2. Who gives life to every person? _____
    _____

3. What special person was going to be one of Abraham's descendants? _____
    _____

4. Was Abraham a sinner? _____

5. When did God give Abraham the gift of righteousness? _____
    _____
    _____

6. What did God tell Abraham would happen to his descendants after his death? _____
    _____
    _____
    _____
    _____

7. Why did God wait four hundred years to give the land of Canaan to Abraham's
    descendants? _____
    _____

8. Who is the only One who can make you acceptable to God? _____
    _____

9. Who did God promise to send to rescue you from sin and death_____
    _____

10. What is the only way for you to please God? _____
    _____
    _____

(Answers in *The Most Amazing Story*, pages 133-134)

Lesson 20—**Helpless**

Memory Verse

> *And he believed in the Lord, and He accounted it to him for righteousness.*
> *Genesis 15:6*

Questions

1. After Lot moved away, what did God say He would give to Abraham? _____
   _____
   _____

2. Who gives life to every person? _____
   _____

3. What special person was going to be one of Abraham's descendants? _____
   _____

4. Was Abraham a sinner? _____

5. When did God give Abraham the gift of righteousness? _____
   _____
   _____

6. What did God tell Abraham would happen to his descendants after his death?
   _____
   _____
   _____

7. Why did God wait four hundred years to give the land of Canaan to Abraham's
   descendants? _____
   _____

8. Who is the only One who can make you acceptable to God? _____
   _____

9. Who did God promise to send to rescue you from sin and death? _____
   _____

10. What is the only way for you to please God? _____
    _____
    _____

(Answers in *The Most Amazing Story*, pages 139-140)

Lesson 21—**Twins**

Memory Verse

I, even I, am the Lord, and besides Me there is no savior. Isaiah 43:11

Questions

1. Why were the twins fighting inside Rebekah? _____
   _____
   _____

2. What promises did God make to Abraham? _____
   _____
   _____

3. Was God going to keep these promises, even though they did not come true during Abraham's lifetime? _____
   _____

4. Who did Abraham pass the promises on to? _____
   _____

5. Did Esau care about God? _____
   _____

6. What did Jacob see in his dream? _____
   _____

7. How does this ladder remind us of the promised Savior? _____
   _____

8. What did God promise Jacob in his dream? _____
   _____
   _____

9. Why is it important for you to think about what will happen to you after you die? __
   _____
   _____
   _____
   _____
   _____

(Answers in *The Most Amazing Story*, pages 147-148)

Lesson 22—**Jealous Brothers**

Memory Verse

There are many plans in a man's heart, nevertheless the LORD's counsel that will stand.
Proverbs 19:21

Questions

1. How did God take care of Jacob in Mesopotamia? _____
_____
_____

2. How many sons did Jacob have? _____

3. Who was Jacob's favorite son? _____
_____

4. Why were Joseph's brothers angry with him? _____
_____
_____
_____

5. What happened in Joseph's dreams? _____
_____
_____
_____

6. Who gave these dreams to Joseph? _____
_____

7. What did Joseph's brothers do to him? _____
_____

8. What did Jacob think happened to Joseph? _____
_____

9. What terrible thing happened to Joseph while he was working for Potiphar?
_____
_____

10. Did Joseph stop trusting God because of all the terrible things that happened to him?
_____
_____

(Answers in *The Most Amazing Story*, page 155)

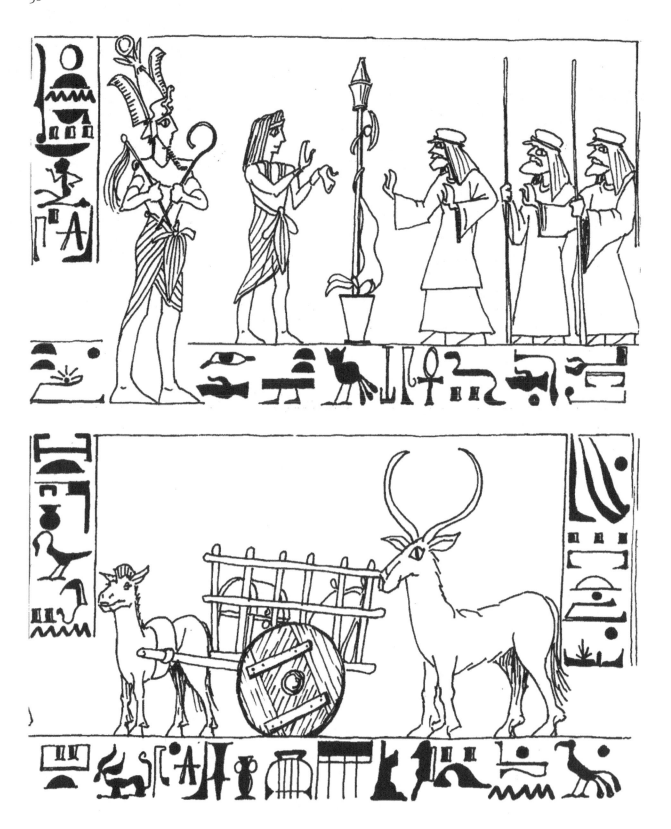

Lesson 23—The King's Dreams

Memory Verse

> *There are many plans in a man's heart, nevertheless the LORD's counsel that will stand.*
> *Proverbs 19:21*

Questions

1. What did the king of Egypt dream? _____
   _____
   _____
   _____
   _____

2. What did Pharaoh's dreams mean? _____
   _____
   _____

3. Who showed Joseph the meaning of Pharaoh's dreams? _____
   _____

4. Who protected Joseph from being killed by his brothers? _____
   _____

5. Who protected Joseph while he was in prison? _____
   _____

6. Who caused the pharaoh to bring Joseph out of prison and make him the governor
   of Egypt? _____
   _____
   _____

7. Did the dreams God gave Joseph about his brothers bowing down to him come true?
   _____
   _____

8. How much does God know? _____
   _____
   _____

(Answers in *The Most Amazing Story*, page 162)

Lesson 24—**Suffering in Egypt**

Memory Verse

> *There are many plans in a man's heart, nevertheless the LORD's counsel—that will stand.*
> *Proverbs 19:21*

Questions

1. Why was Joseph not angry with his brothers? _____
   _____
   _____

2. Why did God take special care of Jacob's family? _____
   _____
   _____

3. What was Jacob's other name? _____
   _____

4. Why was the new king of Egypt afraid of the Israelites? _____
   _____
   _____

5. What did the king do to stop the Israelites from increasing in number? _____
   _____
   _____

6. Who was leading the king of Egypt? _____
   _____

7. Why did Satan want to destroy the nation of Israel? _____
   _____
   _____
   _____

8. Could Satan or the pharaoh ruin God's plan to send the Savior? _____
   _____
   _____
   _____
   _____

(Answers in *The Most Amazing Story*, page 167)

Lesson 25—**Rescued by a Princess**

Memory Verse

For the LORD Most High is awesome; He is a great King over all the earth. Psalm 47:2

Questions

1. Why did God take special care to protect baby Moses? _____
    _____
    _____

2. What did Moses see the day he was on the mountain taking care of his father-in-law's
    sheep? _____
    _____

3. In what way was this bush not burning up a picture of what was happening to the
    Israelites? _____
    _____
    _____

4. Why did God tell Moses to stay back and to take off his sandals? _____
    _____
    _____
    _____
    _____

5. Why was God going to free the Israelites from slavery? _____
    _____
    _____
    _____
    _____

6. Did God clearly communicate with Moses? Did Moses know what God wanted him
    to do? _____
    _____

7. Can sinful people live with God in Heaven? _____
    _____

8. Because God loves you so much, who did He promise to send? _____
    _____
    _____
    _____

(Answers in *The Most Amazing Story*, pages 173-174)

Lesson 26—**I AM**

Memory Verse

> *The king's heart is in the hand of the LORD, like the rivers of water; He turns it wherever He wishes. Proverbs 21:1*

Questions

1. To which mountain did God tell Moses He would bring the Israelites after He freed them from slavery in Egypt? _____
    _____
    _____

2. What does the name I AM tell us about God? _____
    _____
    _____
    _____

3. Did God know Pharaoh would be stubborn about letting the Israelites go? _____
    _____
    _____
    _____

4. What signs did God give Moses to show Moses He was powerful enough to rescue the Israelites from Egypt? _____
    _____
    _____

5. After these three signs, did Moses finally believe God? _____
    _____
    _____

6. Why did God become angry with Moses? _____
    _____
    _____

7. How did God show mercy to Moses? _____

8. Does God have all power to do whatever He says He will do? _____
    _____

9. Does God always tell the truth?_____

10. Does God love you? _____
    _____

11. What is the only way to please God? _____
    _____

(Answers in *The Most Amazing Story*, pages 180)

Lesson 27—**Let My People Go**

Memory Verse

The king's heart is in the hand of the LORD, like the rivers of water; He turns it wherever He wishes. Proverbs 21:1

Questions

1. Did Pharaoh and the Egyptians worship the one true and living God? _____
    _____
    _____

2. Could Pharaoh and Satan stop God from freeing the Israelites? _____
    _____
    _____

3. Did God know Pharaoh would be stubborn and not let the Israelites go? _____
    _____
    _____

4. Can you name some of the plagues God sent on Egypt? _____
    _____
    _____
    _____
    _____
    _____
    _____

5. What did the plagues show about the God of Israel?_____
    _____
    _____

6. Can anyone defeat God's plans? _____
    _____
    _____
    _____
    _____

(Answers in *The Most Amazing Story*, pages 188)

Lesson 28—When I See the Blood

Memory Verse

> *Now the blood shall be a sign for you on the houses where you are. And when I see the blood, I will pass over you [...] Exodus 12:13a*

Questions

1. What was the last plague God sent on Egypt? _____
   _____
   _____

2. What did God tell the Israelites to do in order to save their sons from death? _____
   _____
   _____

3. If an Israelite would have sacrificed a lamb that had sores or was sick, would God have saved the firstborn son in that family? _____
   _____
   _____

4. Why were the Israelites not to break any of the lamb's bones? _____
   _____
   _____

5. After they sprinkled the blood on the doorframes, where were the Israelites to go?__
   _____
   _____

6. Would God enter any home where the blood of the lamb had been sprinkled on the doorframe? _____
   _____
   _____

7. Why did the Israelites carefully follow God's instructions? _____
   _____
   _____
   _____

8. Why was the night the Israelites were to remember each year called the Passover Feast? _____
   _____
   _____

(Answers in *The Most Amazing Story*, pages 195)

Lesson 29—**Trapped**

Memory Verse

> *Now the blood shall be a sign for you on the houses where you are. And when I see the blood, I will pass over you [...] Exodus 12:13a*

Questions

1. Did God give Abraham countless descendants like He promised? _____
   _____
   _____

2. How did God lead the Israelites through the wilderness? _____
   _____

3. When the Israelites left Egypt, where were they going? _____
   _____

4. When the Israelites saw the Egyptian army coming after them, did they trust God to take care of them? _____
   _____
   _____

5. Was there any way for the Israelites to save themselves from the Egyptians? _____
   _____
   _____
   _____

6. Who was the only One who could save the Israelites from the Egyptian army? _____
   _____

7. What did God do to save the Israelites? _____
   _____
   _____
   _____
   _____

8. How could God make a dry path through the sea? _____
   _____
   _____

9. Is there anything you can do to save yourself from sin and death? _____
   _____

10. Who is the only One who can save you? _____

11. Who did God promise to send to make a way for all people to be saved from sin and death? _____

(Answers in *The Most Amazing Story*, page 203)

Lesson 30—**Hungry and Thirsty**

Memory Verse

> *But to him who does not work but believes on Him who justifies the ungodly, his faith is accounted for righteousness, Romans 4:5*

Questions

1. When the Israelites were hungry and thirsty in the wilderness, did they trust God to provide for them? _____
   _____

2. What had God done for the Israelites to free them from slavery in Egypt? _____
   _____

3. What did God do for the Israelites when they were trapped between Pharaoh's army and the Red Sea? _____
   _____

4. What land did God promise to give to Abraham's descendants? _____
   _____

5. Since the Israelites knew God had promised to give them the land of Canaan, and since they had seen how powerful God is, should they have worried and complained?
   _____

6. Who was the only One who could provide food and water for over two million Israelites and all their animals in the middle of that endless and empty wilderness?
   _____
   _____

7. Did God get angry with the Israelites for not trusting Him? _____
   _____

8. What did God do for the Israelites when they grumbled about not having food and water? _____

9. Did God make the Israelites promise never to complain again before He would give them food and water? _____

10. Who is the only One who can give you what you need so that you can live and not die and be separated from God forever? _____
    _____

11. What does God ask you to do so you can be saved from eternal death? _____
    _____
    _____
    _____
    _____

(Answers in *The Most Amazing Story*, pages 209-210)

Lesson 31—**A New Agreement**

Memory Verse

> *But to him who does not work but believes on Him who justifies the ungodly, his faith is accounted for righteousness, Romans 4:5*

Questions

1. Did God keep His promise to free the Israelites from slavery and bring them to the mountain where Moses saw the burning bush? _____ _____ _____

2. Explain the agreement God made with the Israelites. _____ _____ _____

3. Did the Israelites think they could obey God's commands? _____ _____

4. Why did God say for the Israelites to wash their clothes? _____ _____ _____

5. What did God say would happen to anyone who touched the mountain where He was? _____

6. Why were Moses and the people so afraid when God came down? _____ _____ _____

7. Is anyone more powerful and majestic than God? _____ _____

8. Can anyone please God by being good? _____ _____ _____

9. Who is the only One who can clean you from your sin and make you acceptable to God so you can live with Him forever? _____ _____ _____ _____

(Answers in *The Most Amazing Story*, page 216)

Lesson 32—**Ten Rules**

Memory Verse

> *For whoever shall keep the whole law, and yet stumble in one point, he is guilty of all.*
> *James 2:10*

Questions

1. What did the Israelites have to do so God would keep treating them as His special treasure? _____

2. Why is it wrong to worship other gods? _____
    _____
    _____

3. What do the Ten Commandments show us? _____
    _____

4. Is it right to use God's name as a swear word? _____
    _____

5. What did God mean when He said to honor your father and your mother? _____
    _____
    _____
    _____

6. Is it wrong to be angry with someone? _____
    _____
    _____
    _____

7. What was the last command God gave? _____
    _____

8. How are God's commands like a mirror? _____
    _____

9. What is the penalty for breaking God's commands? _____
    _____

10. What happens if you only break one command? _____
    _____
    _____
    _____

11. Who is the only One who can make you acceptable to God and save you from the death penalty you deserve? _____
    _____
    _____

(Answers in *The Most Amazing Story*, pages 223-224)

Lesson 33—**A Broken Agreement**

Memory Verse

> *For whoever shall keep the whole law, and yet stumble in one point, he is guilty of all.*
> *James 2:10*

Questions

1. What was the first command God gave the Israelites? _____
   _____

2. What was the second command? _____
   _____

3. Why did God write His rules on tablets of stone? _____
   _____
   _____

4. While Moses was up on the mountain getting the stone tablets, what did the
   Israelites ask Aaron to do? _____
   _____

5. Do man-made gods have any power? _____
   _____

6. Did Aaron do what the people asked? _____
   _____

7. What did the people say about the calf? _____
   _____

8. Did God know what the people were doing? _____

9. What happened to the Israelites because of this sin?_____
   _____

10. In what way are you like the Israelites? _____
    _____

11. Who is the only One who can save you from eternal separation from God? _____
    _____
    _____
    _____

(Answers in *The Most Amazing Story*, pages 230-231)

Lesson 34—**A Beautiful Tent**

Memory Verse

The LORD is great in Zion, and He is high above all the peoples. Let them praise Your great and awesome name—He is holy. Psalm 99:2-3

Questions

1. Did the Israelites keep their agreement with God to obey all His rules? _____
    _____
    _____

2. What is the penalty for breaking God's rules? _____
    _____
    _____

3. What did God tell the Israelites to build so He could come live in their camp? _____
    _____
    _____

4. Did God tell the Israelites how to build the tabernacle? _____
    _____
    _____

5. What two rooms did God tell Moses to put inside the tabernacle? _____
    _____

6. Where did God tell Moses to put the Ark of the Testimony? _____
    _____

7. When God came to live in the tabernacle, where was He going to live? _____
    _____

8. Why were the Israelites careful to build everything exactly the way God told them
    to? _____
    _____

9. What would have happened if the Israelites would not have built the tabernacle
    exactly as God said? _____
    _____

10. Is there anything you can do to make God accept you? _____
    _____
    _____
    _____

11. How does God want you to come to Him to be forgiven of your sin? _____
    _____

(Answers in *The Most Amazing Story*, page 238)

Lesson 35—**Forgiveness**

Memory Verse

The LORD is great in Zion, and He is high above all the peoples. Let them praise Your great and awesome name—He is holy. Psalm 99:2-3

Questions

1. Why did God want the priests to wash before serving Him in the tabernacle? _____
   _____
   _____
   _____

2. Where in the tabernacle did God live? _____
   _____
   _____

3. Whenever an Israelite broke one of God's rules, what did he have to do? _____
   _____
   _____
   _____
   _____

4. What did God mean when He said the offering would make atonement for the person?
   _____

5. Why did the high priest take the blood of a special sacrifice into the Most Holy Place once a year? _____
   _____
   _____

6. In what way were the Israelites reminded every day that the payment for sin is death?
   _____
   _____
   _____

7. What happens to sinful people when they die? _____
   _____
   _____

8. Is there any way to escape this terrible penalty? _____
   _____
   _____

(Answers in *The Most Amazing Story*, page 244)

Lesson 36—**Spies**

Memory Verse

So we see that they could not enter in because of unbelief. Hebrews 3:19

Questions

1. What was the land called that God promised to give to Abraham and his descendants?
    _____

2. What were the people in Canaan like? _____
    _____

3. What good things did the spies find in the land of Canaan? _____
    _____
    _____

4. Why were the spies scared of the people of Canaan? _____
    _____

5. Who did most of the spies think was more powerful – God or the giant Canaanites?
    _____

6. What did the people do when they heard there were giants in Canaan? _____
    _____
    _____

7. Which two spies believed God? _____
    _____

8. Why should the Israelites have believed God? _____
    _____
    _____
    _____
    _____

9. What did God do when the people did not believe Him? _____
    _____
    _____
    _____

10. What is the only way to please God? _____
    _____
    _____
    _____
    _____

(Answers in *The Most Amazing Story*, page 244)

Lesson 37—**Snakes**

Memory Verse

So we see that they could not enter in because of unbelief. Hebrews 3:19

Questions

1. What did God tell Moses to do to the rock so the Israelites could have water? _____
   _____

2. Did Moses do what God said? _____
   _____

3. Why did God tell Moses and Aaron they could not lead the Israelites into the land of
   Canaan? _____
   _____
   _____
   _____

4. What is the end result of sin? _____

5. Why did God send poisonous snakes to bite the Israelites? _____
   _____

6. What did the Israelites do when many of them died from the snake bites? _____
   _____

7. Who was the only One who could save the Israelites from death? _____
   _____

8. Did the snake on the pole have special power to save the Israelites? _____
   _____

9. Besides looking up at the snake on the pole, what else did God ask the Israelites to
   do in order to be saved? _____
   _____

10. Who is the only One who can save you from the death you deserve for your sin? ___
    _____

11. Is there anything you can do to help God save you? _____
    _____
    _____

(Answers in *The Most Amazing Story*, pages 257-258)

Lesson 38—**Canaan at Last**

Memory Verse

Great is our Lord, and mighty in power; His understanding is infinite. Psalm 147:5

Questions

1. Did God give the land of Canaan to the Israelites because of how good they were? __
   _____

2. Since God did not give Canaan to the Israelites because of their good behavior, why did He give the land to Israel? _____
   _____
   _____

3. How did God show His love to Moses before Moses died? _____
   _____

4. After Moses died, who did God choose to be the next leader of Israel? _____
   _____

5. Were the Israelites strong enough to defeat the Canaanites? _____
   _____

6. Who was the only One who could defeat the Canaanites and give their land to the people of Israel? _____
   _____

7. What did God tell the Israelites to do at Jericho? _____
   _____
   _____
   _____

8. Because the Israelites believed God and followed His commands, what happened to the city of Jericho? _____
   _____

9. Did God keep His promise to Abraham to give the land of Canaan to his descendants?
   _____

10. Who is the only One who can rescue you from your sin, Satan, and the death penalty?
    _____
    _____

(Answers in *The Most Amazing Story*, page 264)

Lesson 39—**False Gods**

Memory Verse

Great is our Lord, and mighty in power; His understanding is infinite. Psalm 147:5

Questions

1. Did God always take care of the Israelites? _____
_____

2. What did God warn the Israelites would happen if they broke their agreement with Him? _____
_____
_____

3. What did the people do after Joshua died? _____
_____

4. Does God always do what He says He will do? _____
_____
_____

5. Whenever the Israelites called out to God to save them, what did He do? _____
_____
_____

6. What happened every time the judge died? _____
_____

7. Who was the woman God used to deliver the Israelites from the Canaanite king, Jabin?
_____
_____

8. What does the word mercy mean? _____
_____

9. What do you deserve for breaking God's rules? _____
_____
_____

10. Who did God promise to send to rescue you from the death penalty you deserve? __
_____
_____

(Answers in *The Most Amazing Story*, page 272)

Lesson 40—**A Trumpet and a Pitcher**

Memory Verse

> *Oh, give thanks to the LORD, for He is good! For His mercy endures forever.*
> *Psalm 118:29*

Questions

1. What were the Midianites doing to the Israelites to make them suffer? _____
   _____
   _____

2. How many Midianite people were there? _____
   _____

3. Were the Israelites powerful enough to defeat the Midianites? _____
   _____

4. Even though the Israelites kept turning away from God, did God have mercy on them
   whenever they cried out to Him because of their suffering? _____
   _____
   _____

5. At first, how many Israelite soldiers did Gideon gather to help him fight the
   Midianites? _____
   _____

6. What did God say to Gideon about his large army? _____
   _____
   _____

7. Why did twenty-two thousand of Gideon's men leave? _____
   _____

8. What did God tell Gideon to do next to make even more soldiers leave? _____
   _____
   _____

9. Why did God want Gideon's army to be so small? _____
   _____
   _____

10. Who is the only One who can rescue you from Satan, sin, and death? _____
    _____
    _____
    _____

(Answers in *The Most Amazing Story*, pages 277-280)

Lesson 41—**Tricked**

Memory Verse

> *Oh, give thanks to the LORD, for He is good! For His mercy endures forever.*
> *Psalm 118:29*

Questions

1. How could God give Manoah's wife a baby when she had never been able to have children before? _____
_____
_____

2. What was God's plan for this baby named Samson? _____
_____

3. What was a Nazirite? _____
_____

4. As a Nazirite, what was Samson not allowed to do? _____
_____

5. Who gave Samson his incredible strength? _____

6. How did Samson use his God-given strength to defeat the Philistines? _____
_____
_____

7. Was Samson a sinner? _____
_____

8. What did Samson do that caused him to get caught by the Philistines? _____
_____
_____

9. How did Samson kill more Philistines in his death than he did during his life? _____
_____
_____
_____
_____

10. Who is the only true, living, and powerful God? _____
_____

(Answers in *The Most Amazing Story*, page 289)

Lesson 42—**A Giant**

Memory Verse

But I have trusted in Your mercy; my heart shall rejoice in Your salvation. Psalm 13:5

Questions

1. For what did Hannah pray? _____
    _____

2. What was the promise Hannah made to God? _____
    _____
    _____

3. In what way did Israel reject God? _____
    _____
    _____

4. Who did God choose to be Israel's first king? _____
    _____

5. While Saul was king, who came against the Israelites in battle? _____
    _____
    _____

6. Why were all the Israelite soldiers afraid? _____
    _____

7. Why was the young shepherd boy David not afraid to fight Goliath? ___
    _____
    _____

8. When David became king of Israel, did he lead the Israelites to follow God? _____
    _____
    _____

9. Who did David believe was the only One who could save him from the death penalty
    he deserved for his sin? _____
    _____
    _____
    _____

(Answers in *The Most Amazing Story*, page 300)

Lesson 43—**An Awesome Temple**

Memory Verse

But I have trusted in Your mercy; my heart shall rejoice in Your salvation. Psalm 13:5

Questions

1. Now that the Israelites were at peace with the other nations, what did King David want to do for God? _____

   _____

2. Who did God choose to build a permanent house for Him instead of King David? __

   _____

3. What promise did God make to King David? _____

   _____

   _____

4. What was the house called that King Solomon built for God? _____

   _____

5. What was the capital city of Israel where King Solomon built the temple? _____

   _____

6. In what way was the temple like the tabernacle? _____

   _____

   _____

   _____

   _____

7. Who lived behind the heavy curtain in the Most Holy Place of the temple?_____

   _____

   _____

8. When King Solomon turned away from God, what happened to the nation of Israel?

   _____

   _____

   _____

9. Over which kingdom did King David's family rule? _____

   _____

   _____

(Answers in *The Most Amazing Story*, pages 306-307)

Lesson 44—**Cry Louder!**

Memory Verse

> *[...] for this is good and acceptable in the sight of God our Savior, who desires all men to be saved and to come to the knowledge of the truth... 1Timothy 2:3-4*

Questions

1. Did most of the kings of Israel and Judah follow God? _____
    _____
    _____

2. What were the men called whom God sent to warn the Israelites about the consequences of their sin? _____
    _____
    _____

3. What warning did the prophets give to the Israelites and their kings? _____
    _____
    _____

4. Did God want the Israelites to die? _____
    _____
    _____

5. Does God have the power to control nature? _____
    _____
    _____

6. How did God take care of the widow who helped the prophet Elijah? _____
    _____
    _____

7. What happened when the prophets of Baal called on their god to send down fire? __
    _____
    _____

8. What happened when Elijah called on God to send down fire? _____
    _____
    _____

9. How does God speak to us today? _____

10. What does the Bible say is the penalty for sin?_____

11. How can you be saved from death? _____
    _____

(Answers in *The Most Amazing Story*, pages 314-315)

Lesson 45—**Swallowed by a Fish**

Memory Verse

The Lord is [...] longsuffering toward us, not willing that any should perish but that all should come to repentance. 2 Peter 3:9

Questions

1. What did God's prophets warn the Israelites would happen if they continued to sin?
    _____
    _____
    _____

2. What did the false prophets tell the Israelites? _____
    _____

3. Who sent the false prophets? _____

4. Did God love the Assyrians even though they were not His special people and even though they were wicked and hateful? _____
    _____
    _____

5. Why was Jonah unwilling to go to Nineveh? _____
    _____
    _____

6. Could Jonah hide from God? _____

7. Who finally conquered the northern kingdom of Israel? _____

8. Is everything God says in the Bible true? _____
    _____

9. Is it true that the penalty for sin is separation from God forever in the terrible place of suffering? _____

10. Why does Satan try to trick you with lies like, "There is no God," and "There is no terrible place of suffering"? _____
    _____
    _____
    _____
    _____

(Answers in *The Most Amazing Story*, pages 322-323)

Lesson 46—**A Burning Fiery Furnace**

Memory Verse

> *Look to Me, and be saved, all you ends of the earth! For I am God, and there is no other. Isaiah 45:22*

Questions

1. Why did God allow the nation of Babylon to conquer Judah and destroy the city of Jerusalem? _____
   _____

2. Who gave Daniel, Shadrach, Meshach, and Abed-Nego wisdom and understanding?
   _____
   _____

3. What was King Nebuchadnezzar's command that Shadrach, Meshach, and Abed-Nego refused to follow? _____
   _____
   _____

4. What did the king say would happen to anyone who did not bow down to his image?
   _____
   _____

5. What did Shadrach, Meshach, and Abed-Nego say to King Nebuchadnezzar? _____
   _____
   _____
   _____
   _____

6. What happened to the men who threw the three Israelites into the fire? _____
   _____

7. Who did the king see in the fire with the three Israelites? _____
   _____
   _____

8. Were the three men who were thrown into the fire burned at all? _____

9. What did the king learn about the God of Israel? _____
   _____
   _____

10. Why should you believe God? _____
    _____
    _____

(Answers in *The Most Amazing Story*, pages 330-331)

Lesson 47—**In the Lion's Den**

Memory Verse

Look to Me, and be saved, all you ends of the earth! For I am God, and there is no other. Isaiah 45:22

Questions

1. Who were the four young captives from Judah who believed God? _____
   _____
   _____

2. Which of God's prophets wrote the book of Daniel? _____
   _____

3. Did Nebuchadnezzar, king of the great Babylonian empire, believe in God? _____
   _____
   _____

4. Who conquered Babylon? _____
   _____

5. Who was the king of the Medes and Persians when Babylon was conquered? _____
   _____

6. Could a law of the Medes and Persians be changed? _____
   _____

7. Why were the governors and officials jealous of Daniel? _____
   _____
   _____

8. How did the governors, princes, and supervisors trick the king? _____
   _____
   _____
   _____

9. Did Daniel pray to God even though he knew he would be thrown into the den of lions? _____

10. Did God have the power to save Daniel from the lions? _____
    _____

11. Who is the highest authority in the whole world? _____
    _____

(Answers in *The Most Amazing Story*, pages 337-338)

Lesson 48—**God's Plans**

Memory Verse

> *I, even I, am the LORD, and besides Me there is no savior. Isaiah 43:11*

Questions

1. What did Cyrus, king of Persia, allow some of the Jews do? _____
    _____

2. What were the buildings called where the Jews outside of Jerusalem met to hear God's Word? _____

3. Did the Jewish religious leaders understand the true meaning of what Moses and the prophets wrote in the Old Testament? _____
    _____
    _____

4. Why did the Jews think God accepted them? _____
    _____
    _____

5. Why were the Jews not acceptable to God? _____
    _____

6. Who was the only One who could save the Jews from sin and death and make them acceptable to God? _____
    _____
    _____

7. Into what nation was the Savior going to be born? _____
    _____

8. From whose family line would the Savior come? _____
    _____

9. Where did the prophet Micah say the Savior would be born? _____
    _____

10. What language did almost everyone in the known world speak? _____
    _____

11. What did the Romans build that would help the news about the Savior spread to all people? _____

12. Was the Roman emperor kind to the Jews? _____
    _____

13. Can anyone stop God from doing what He plans to do? _____
    _____

(Answers in *The Most Amazing Story*, pages 343-344)

Lesson 49—**A Special Baby**

Memory Verse

> *Behold, I send My messenger, and he will prepare the way before Me […] Malachi 3:1a*

Questions

1. Did the prophets tell the truth when they said Israel and Judah would be taken captive by their enemies? _____

   _____

2. Who told the prophets what would happen in the future? _____

   _____

   _____

3. Were the prophets careful to write down exactly what God said, or did they write some of their own ideas in the Bible? _____

   _____

   _____

4. Did everything the prophets wrote in the Old Testament about the Savior come true?

   _____

   _____

5. Who did the prophet Malachi say was coming to Earth? _____

   _____

6. Who did Zacharias and Elizabeth believe was the only One who could save them from the death penalty they deserved for their sin? _____

   _____

   _____

7. What did the angel Gabriel say to Zacharias? _____

   _____

   _____

8. Why should Zacharias have believed God? _____

   _____

   _____

9. What did God tell Zacharias and Elizabeth to name their baby? _____

   _____

10. What was God's plan for John? _____

    _____

    _____

(Answers in *The Most Amazing Story*, pages 350-351)

Lesson 50—**Immanuel: God with Us**

Memory Verse

> *"Behold, the virgin shall be with child, and bear a Son, and they shall call His name Immanuel," which is translated, "God with us." Matthew 1:23*

Questions

1. Who did the angel Gabriel appear to this time? _____
    _____

2. What did Gabriel tell Mary? _____
    _____

3. What does the name Jesus mean? _____
    _____

4. What had the prophet Isaiah predicted about the virgin hundreds of years earlier?
    _____
    _____
    _____

5. What does the name Immanuel mean? _____
    _____

6. How would the baby Jesus be different from every other person born into the world?
    _____
    _____
    _____

7. Could an imperfect Savior rescue you and me from Satan's dominion and from the death penalty we deserve for our sin? _____
    _____

8. What does the name Christ (or Messiah) mean? _____
    _____
    _____

9. What were the three special jobs God planned for the Messiah, Jesus, to do? _____
    _____
    _____

10. From the very beginning, who did God plan to send to Earth to rescue us from Satan and make us acceptable to Him? _____
    _____
    _____

(Answers in *The Most Amazing Story*, pages 357-358)

Lesson 51—**A Preacher In the Desert**

Memory Verse

For there is born to you this day in the city of David a Savior, who is Christ the Lord. Luke 2:11

Questions

1. Did God give Zacharias and Elizabeth a baby like the angel said He would? _____
   _____
   _____

2. What happened to Zacharias when he wrote the baby's name on the tablet of paper?
   _____

3. What did John tell the people of Israel to do in order to get ready for the coming of
   the Savior? _____
   _____
   _____
   _____
   _____

4. Did getting baptized in water make the Jews acceptable to God? _____
   _____

5. Who were the three groups of religious leaders in Israel? _____
   _____

6. Why did John call the religious leaders a "brood of vipers"? _____
   _____
   _____
   _____
   _____

7. How does God feel about sin? _____
   _____
   _____

8. What does God want you to change your mind about? _____
   _____
   _____
   _____
   _____
   _____

9. What will happen to those who do not trust in the Savior to save them? _____
   _____
   _____

(Answers in *The Most Amazing Story*, page 365)

Lesson 52—**Good News for Everyone**

Memory Verse

> *For there is born to you this day in the city of David a Savior, who is Christ the Lord. Luke 2:11*

Questions

1. Why did Joseph and Mary go to Bethlehem? _____
    _____

2. Whose family line was Joseph from? _____

3. What important event happened while Joseph and Mary were in Bethlehem? _____
    _____

4. Were the people of Israel waiting for the Savior to be born? _____
    _____
    _____

5. Who told the shepherds about the Savior's birth? _____
    _____

6. Was baby Jesus, God the Son, born in a hospital? _____
    _____

7. How did the scribes know where the King of the Jews was to be born? _____
    _____
    _____

8. Was King Herod happy that a king was born in Bethlehem? _____
    _____

9. What did King Herod do to all the babies around Bethlehem? _____
    _____

10. How did baby Jesus escape being killed by Herod's soldiers? _____
    _____

11. Did God know Satan would try to hurt Jesus? _____
    _____
    _____

12. Did everything the prophets predicted about Jesus come to pass? _____
    _____

13. Who was in control of Jesus' life? *God was.* _____
    _____

14. Where did Jesus grow up? _____

15. Did Jesus ever do anything wrong when He was growing up? _____
    _____

(Answers in *The Most Amazing Story*, pages 372-373)

Lesson 53—**God's Lamb**

Memory Verse

The next day John saw Jesus coming toward him, and said, "Behold! The Lamb of God who takes away the sin of the world!" John 1:29

Questions

1. Why did Jesus want John the Baptist to baptize Him? _____
    _____

2. Who came to be with Jesus to give Him strength and wisdom to accomplish God's work on Earth? _____
    _____

3. What did God the Father say about Jesus when He came out of the water after John baptized Him? _____
    _____
    _____

4. Has any other person ever been pleasing to God like Jesus was? _____
    _____
    _____
    _____

5. How did John recognize Jesus as the promised Savior? _____
    _____
    _____
    _____

6. Up until now, how could an Israelite who broke God's command be saved from death?
    _____
    _____
    _____
    _____

7. What did John the Baptist say about Jesus? _____
    _____

8. Who did God provide to rescue you from the death penalty you deserve? _____
    _____
    _____
    _____

(Answers in *The Most Amazing Story*, pages 378-379)

Lesson 54—**Satan Tries to Trick Jesus**

Memory Verse

> *The next day John saw Jesus coming toward him, and said, "Behold! The Lamb of God who takes away the sin of the world!" John 1:29*

Questions

1. Why did Jesus not turn the stones into bread like Satan asked him to do? _____
    _____
    _____
    _____

2. What did Jesus say is more important than food? _____
    _____
    _____

3. Why is the Bible more important than food? _____
    _____
    _____

4. Why did Satan want Jesus to jump off the roof of the temple? _____
    _____
    _____
    _____

5. Why is it wrong to test God to see if He is telling the truth? _____
    _____
    _____
    _____

6. Why do the kingdoms of the world belong to Satan? _____
    _____
    _____
    _____

7. Who was the Child of a woman who would bruise Satan's head? _____
    _____
    _____

8. Every time Satan tried to get Jesus to do what he said, what did Jesus tell Satan? ___
    _____
    _____

9. Did Jesus ever do what Satan told Him to do? _____
    _____
    _____

(Answers in *The Most Amazing Story*, page 385)

Lesson 55—**Jesus Teaches and Heals**

Memory Verse

> *Nor is there salvation in any other, for there is no other name under heaven given among men by which we must be saved. Acts 4:12*

Questions

1. What did King Herod do to John the Baptist? _____
_____

2. What was the good news for the Israelites? _____
_____
_____

3. The name Christ, or Messiah, means Chosen One. Why was Jesus called God's Chosen One? What was He chosen to do? _____
_____

4. What did Jesus mean when He said He would make the disciples fishers of men? ___
_____
_____
_____

5. Did the scribes know what was written in God's Word? _____
_____

6. Why were the people in the synagogue amazed at Jesus' teaching? _____
_____
_____

7. Why could Jesus explain God's Word so well? _____
_____

8. Why did Jesus have the power to make demons leave out of people? _____
_____
_____

9. Who was the only One who could heal the man with leprosy? _____
_____

10. Did Jesus stay away from the man with leprosy like everyone else did? _____
_____

11. In what way are you like the man who had leprosy? _____
_____
_____
_____
_____

(Answers in *The Most Amazing Story*, pages 394-395)

Lesson 56—**A Visitor at Night**

Memory Verse

Nor is there salvation in any other, for there is no other name under heaven given among men by which we must be saved. Acts 4:12

Questions

1. Why do you think Nicodemus came to Jesus at night? _____
    _____
    _____
    _____

2. What made the Pharisees think they were acceptable to God? _____
    _____

3. Into whose family were the Pharisees really born? _____
    _____
    _____

4. When God looks at mankind, what two kinds of people does He see? _____
    _____
    _____
    _____

5. If you are in Adam's family, is your spirit dead or alive to God? _____
    _____

6. Who is the only One who can give life to your spirit and place you into God's family?
    _____
    _____

7. When the Israelites were bitten by the snakes in the wilderness, was there anything they could do to be saved from death? _____
    _____
    _____

8. Who did Jesus say was going to be hung on a pole? _____
    _____

9. What did Jesus promise would happen to everyone who believes in Him? _____
    _____
    _____
    _____

10. Why did the Jews not want Jesus to shine His light on their sin? _____
    _____
    _____

(Answers in *The Most Amazing Story*, page 401)

Lesson 57—**Two Sick Men**

Memory Verse

> *In the beginning was the Word, and the Word was with God, and the Word was God. John 1:1*

Questions

1. Why did most of the Jews not accept Jesus as their Savior? _____
   _____
   _____
   _____

2. Even though most of the Jews did not want to accept Jesus as their Savior, what did they want Him to do? _____
   _____
   _____

3. Why were the Pharisees and religious leaders jealous of Jesus? _____
   _____

4. What does it mean to blaspheme? _____
   _____
   _____

5. Were the scribes right when they said only God can forgive sins? _____

6. Why was it not wrong for Jesus to tell the man his sins were forgiven? _____
   _____
   _____

7. How could Jesus heal the paralyzed man just by speaking? _____
   _____
   _____
   _____

8. What kind of people did Jesus say need a doctor? _____

9. Why did the Pharisees not come to Jesus to be "healed"? _____
   _____
   _____

10. In what way does God say you are sick?_____
    _____
    _____

11. Who is the only One who can cure you so you won't die?_____
    _____
    _____

(Answers in *The Most Amazing Story*, page 408)

Lesson 58—**Hypocrites**

Memory Verse

In the beginning was the Word, and the Word was with God, and the Word was God. John 1:1

Questions

1. What rule did the Pharisees make up about the Sabbath, or Saturday? _____
   _____

2. Did Jesus obey the laws of the Pharisees?_____

3. What is a hypocrite? _____
   _____

4. In what way were the Pharisees like a dish that was washed on the outside, but was still dirty on the inside? _____
   _____
   _____

5. Why were the Pharisees angry with Jesus? _____
   _____
   _____

6. How could Jesus heal the man's hand just by speaking? _____
   _____
   _____

7. Why was Jesus angry with the Pharisees? _____
   _____
   _____
   _____
   _____
   _____

8. In what way were the Pharisees like the pharaoh of Egypt? _____
   _____
   _____

9. What did the Pharisees and the Herodians want to do to Jesus? _____
   _____

10. How did the demons know who Jesus was? _____

11. Can keeping the Ten Commandments, reading the Bible, or doing good deeds make you acceptable to God? _____
    _____
    _____

12. Who is the only One who can make you acceptable to God? _____
    _____
    _____

(Answers in *The Most Amazing Story*, pages 414-415)

Lesson 59—**Supernatural Power**

Memory Verse

> *Therefore if the Son makes you free, you shall be free indeed. John 8:36*

Questions

1. If Jesus is God, why did Jesus get tired at the end of the day? _____
   _____
   _____
   _____

2. Why were the disciples surprised when the wind and the sea obeyed Jesus? _____
   _____
   _____
   _____

3. Who was the only One who could rescue the demon-possessed man? _____
   _____
   _____
   _____

4. How did the demons cause the man to act? _____
   _____
   _____

5. Did the demons know who Jesus was? _____
   _____
   _____
   _____

6. Why did the demons have to ask permission from Jesus to go into the pigs? _____
   _____
   _____

7. After Jesus freed the man from the demons, what did He want the man to do? _____
   _____
   _____

8. Who is the only One who can rescue you from Satan's dominion and place you into God's family? _____
   _____
   _____

(Answers in *The Most Amazing Story*, page 422)

Lesson 60—**Bread that Gives Eternal Life**

Memory Verse

"I am the living bread which came down from heaven. If anyone eats of this bread, he will live forever;" John 6:51a

Questions

1. What did the crowds want from Jesus? _____
    _____
    _____
    _____

2. Why did Jesus ask Philip how they could feed the crowd? _____
    _____
    _____

3. In what ways did Jesus prove He was God? _____
    _____
    _____
    _____

4. What did the apostle John say about the amount of great and incredible things Jesus did? _____
    _____
    _____

5. When the people saw the great miracles Jesus did, who did they think Jesus was? ___
    _____
    _____
    _____

6. Did the Jews want Jesus to save them from Satan's dominion and the death penalty they deserved for their sin? _____
    _____
    _____
    _____

7. What kind of food did Jesus tell the Jews they should be seeking? _____
    _____
    _____

8. Who is the bread of life who came down from Heaven? _____
    _____
    _____
    _____

(Answers in *The Most Amazing Story*, page 430)

Lesson 61—**Dirty on the Inside**

Memory Verse

So they said, "Believe on the Lord Jesus Christ, and you will be saved [...]" Acts16:31

Questions

1. Why were the Pharisees upset with Jesus' disciples? _____
   _____

2. What was more important to the Pharisees than loving God and loving people? ____
   _____

3. Could the Pharisees make themselves clean on the inside by washing their hands
   before eating? _____
   _____

4. Could the Pharisees make themselves acceptable to God by keeping rules? _____
   _____

5. What makes a person dirty on the inside? _____
   _____

6. How were the Pharisees like Cain? _____
   _____
   _____
   _____

7. How was the tax collector who prayed in the temple like Abel? _____
   _____

8. Can you make yourself acceptable to God by going to church, praying, being baptized,
   or doing good deeds? _____

9. Who is the only One who can make you acceptable to God? _____
   _____
   _____

(Answers in *The Most Amazing Story*, pages 438-439)

Lesson 62—**Who Is Jesus?**

Memory Verse

So they said, "Believe on the Lord Jesus Christ, and you will be saved [...]" Acts16:31

Questions

1. The Jews knew Jesus was someone special because of the miracles He did. Who did they think Jesus was? _____
    _____

2. Who did Peter think Jesus was? _____
    _____

3. What did Jesus say was going to happen to Him? _____
    _____
    _____

4. Even though Jesus looked like any other man, what was different about Him? _____
    _____

5. What happened to Jesus on the mountain? _____
    _____
    _____

6. Why were Moses and Elijah in Heaven with God? _____
    _____
    _____
    _____

7. What were Jesus, Moses, and Elijah talking about up on the mountain? _____
    _____

8. What did God the Father say about Jesus when Jesus was transfigured? _____
    _____
    _____

9. What proofs do we have that Jesus is who He said He was?
    1. _____
    2. _____
    _____
    3. _____
    _____

10. Is it important what you believe about Jesus? _____
    _____
    _____
    _____
    _____

(Answers in *The Most Amazing Story*, pages 446-447)

Lesson 63—**The Good Shepherd**

Memory Verse

I am the good shepherd. The good shepherd gives His life for the sheep. John 10:11

Questions

1. Why did shepherds build sheepfolds? _____
   _____
   _____

2. How many openings, or doorways, did the shepherd make in the sheepfold? _____
   _____
   _____

3. Where did the shepherd sleep at night? _____
   _____

4. What would a good shepherd do if a robber or wild animal tried to get through the
   door of the sheepfold? _____
   _____
   _____

5. How is God's sheepfold like the sheepfold the shepherds built for the sheep? _____
   _____
   _____

6. Who is the thief who comes to steal and kill and destroy? _____
   _____
   _____
   _____

7. In what way is Jesus like the good shepherd who slept in the doorway of the sheepfold?
   _____
   _____
   _____

8. How many doors are there into God's place of safety? _____
   _____
   _____
   _____
   _____

(Answers in *The Most Amazing Story*, page 453)

132

Lesson 64—**Little Children**

Memory Verse

Jesus answered and said to them, "This is the work of God, that you believe in Him whom He sent." John 6:29

Questions

1. Does Jesus care about children _____
   _____
   _____

2. In what way did the Jews need to be like little children?_____
   _____
   _____
   _____

3. Is it true that some people are good and others are bad?_____
   _____
   _____

4. Who is the only One who is good? _____
   _____
   _____

5. How did the rich young man who came running up to Jesus think he could earn eternal life? _____
   _____
   _____

6. What did Jesus tell the man to do? _____
   _____
   _____

7. Why did this man not want to do what Jesus said? _____
   _____
   _____

8. How good did Jesus say the man would have to be in order to earn eternal life? ____
   _____
   _____
   _____

9. What does God want you to be humble about? _____
   _____
   _____
   _____
   _____

(Answers in *The Most Amazing Story*, pages 459-460)

Lesson 65—**Riches are Tricky**

Memory Verse

> *Jesus answered and said to them, "This is the work of God, that you believe in Him whom He sent." John 6:29*

Questions

1. How were the Pharisees hypocrites? _____
_____
_____
_____

2. What happened to the successful farmer in Jesus' parable? _____
_____
_____

3. When you die, can you take your riches with you? _____
_____
_____

4. Can riches give you eternal life? _____
_____

5. Who is the only One who can give eternal life? _____
_____

6. Can riches buy happiness and peace? _____
_____

7. Why did the rich man in Jesus' story go to the place of suffering?_____
_____
_____

8. Why did Lazarus go to paradise when he died? _____
_____
_____

9. After a person goes to the place of suffering, is there any way of escape? _____
_____
_____

10. Why did Abraham say it was useless to send Lazarus to the rich man's brothers to warn them about the terrible place of suffering? _____
_____
_____
_____

(Answers in *The Most Amazing Story*, pages 466-467)

Lesson 66—**A Dead Man Comes Back to Life**

Memory Verse

Jesus said to her, "I am the resurrection and the life. He who believes in Me, though he may die, he shall live." John 11:25

Questions

1. Why did Jesus not heal Lazarus of his sickness? _____
    _____
    _____

2. Did Martha believe Jesus could raise Lazarus from the dead? _____
    _____

3. Did Martha believe Jesus was God the Son, the promised Savior? _____
    _____

4. In the beginning when God created people, did He plan for them to die? _____
    _____
    _____

5. What will happen to those who do not trust in Jesus while they are alive on Earth? _
    _____
    _____
    _____

6. What is the second death? _____
    _____
    _____

7. Did the Jews believe Jesus was God the Son? _____
    _____
    _____

8. What did Jesus do that caused many of the Jews to believe in Him? _____
    _____
    _____

9. Were the Pharisees happy about the Jews believing in Jesus? _____
    _____

10. Who is the only One who can save you from the second death and give you eternal life? _____
    _____
    _____

(Answers in *The Most Amazing Story*, pages 476-477)

Lesson 67—**The Last Passover**

Memory Verse

All we like sheep have gone astray; we have turned, every one, to his own way; and the LORD has laid on Him the iniquity of us all. Isaiah 53:6

Questions

1. Why did God want the Jews to celebrate the Passover Feast? _____
   _____
   _____

2. Why was Jesus sometimes called the Son of Man? _____
   _____
   _____

3. Why did Jesus go to Jerusalem when He knew what was going to happen to Him there?__
   _____
   _____

4. Who was leading Judas and the religious leaders to kill Jesus? _____
   _____
   _____

5. How did Jesus know where the disciples could find a colt for Him to ride? _____

6. Why did the Jews want Jesus to be their king? _____
   _____

7. Why did the Jews not accept Jesus as the promised Savior? _____
   _____
   _____
   _____

8. Did the religious leaders know what was written in the Old Testament about the promised
   Savior? _____

9. Why did the religious leaders want to kill Jesus? _____
   _____
   _____

10. Did Judas trust in Jesus as His Savior? _____
    _____

11. When Jesus was eating the Passover meal with the disciples, why did He break the bread
    and give it to them? _____
    _____

12. What did the cup of wine Jesus gave His disciples at the Passover supper represent? _____
    _____
    _____

(Answers in *The Most Amazing Story*, pages 483-484)

Lesson 68—**Condemned**

Memory Verse

> *All we like sheep have gone astray; we have turned, every one, to his own way; and the LORD has laid on Him the iniquity of us all. Isaiah 53:6*

Questions

1. How did Jesus know everything that was going to happen to Him before it happened?
    _____
    _____
    _____

2. What did Jesus mean when he asked God the Father, "Take this cup away from Me"?
    _____
    _____

3. Even though as a human being Jesus dreaded taking the sin of the world on Himself, was He willing to do whatever God the Father asked Him to do? _____
    _____

4. During His lifetime, did Jesus ever do anything wrong? _____
    _____

5. What did Jesus say when Pilate asked Him if He was the Christ? _____
    _____

6. Why did the Jews get angry when Jesus answered their question about Him being God's Son with, "I am"? _____
    _____
    _____
    _____

7. What did the religious leaders say was the punishment Jesus deserved for calling Himself God? _____
    _____

8. What did Jesus do when He was accused of things He never did? _____
    _____

9. Was it true that Jesus was the King of the Jews? _____
    _____

10. Could Satan destroy God's plans? _____
    _____
    _____
    _____
    _____

11. Did everything the prophets wrote about the Savior in the Old Testament come true?
    _____

(Answers in *The Most Amazing Story*, pages 493-494)

Lesson 69—**Executed**

Memory Verse

> *Christ has redeemed us from the curse of the law, having become a curse for us (for it is written, "Cursed is everyone who hangs on a tree"), Galatians 3:13*

Questions

1. What did Jesus tell Nicodemus that showed He knew how He was going to die? _____
    _____
    _____
    _____

2. Why did the Romans put a sign above the head of criminals who were crucified? ____
    _____
    _____

3. What did the sign above Jesus' head say? _____

4. What do the names "Messiah" and "Christ" tell us about Jesus? _____
    _____
    _____
    _____

5. How was Jesus God's prophet? _____
    _____

6. How could God fulfill His plan for Jesus to be king if He was killed? _____
    _____
    _____
    _____

7. How did the religious leaders make fun of Jesus on the cross? _____
    _____

8. Why did Jesus choose not to come down from the cross? _____
    _____

9. Why did it become as dark as night for three hours while Jesus was on the cross? ____
    _____
    _____
    _____
    _____

10. What did Jesus mean when He said, *"It is finished"* right before He died? _____
    _____
    _____
    _____

(Answers in *The Most Amazing Story*, pages 500-501)

Lesson 70—**Alive**

Memory Verse

He is not here, but is risen! Remember how He spoke to you when He was still in Galilee, saying, "The Son of Man must be delivered into the hands of sinful men, and be crucified, and the third day rise again." Luke 24:6-7

Questions

1. Who asked Pilate for permission to take Jesus' body down from the cross? _____
   _____
   _____

2. Was Joseph rich or poor? _____
   _____

3. In whose tomb was Jesus buried? _____
   _____

4. Who brought a hundred pounds of spices to put on Jesus' body? _____
   _____
   _____

5. Why did the Jewish religious leaders want Pilate to put soldiers by the tomb? _____
   _____
   _____

6. Could anyone stop Jesus from coming back to life? _____
   _____

7. When the women went to Jesus' tomb on Sunday morning, what did they find? ____
   _____
   _____

8. When they realized Jesus' body was gone, what did the religious leaders tell the
   soldiers to say about it? _____
   _____
   _____

9. What proof did God give us that Jesus really did come back to life? _____
   _____
   _____
   _____

10. Before Jesus went back up to Heaven, what did He tell His disciples to do? _____
    _____

11. Will Jesus be king on Earth someday? _____
    _____
    _____

(Answers in *The Most Amazing Story*, pages 509-510)

Lesson 71—**Accepted**

Memory Verse

[...] to the praise of the glory of His grace, by which He made us accepted in the Beloved.
Ephesians 1:6

Questions

1. Were Adam and Eve acceptable to God when He first made them? _____
   _____
   _____

2. What happened to Adam and Eve when they believed Satan instead of God and ate
   from the Tree of the Knowledge of Good and Evil? _____
   _____
   _____

3. After Adam and Eve became sinners, were they still acceptable to God? _____
   _____
   _____

4. How did God make acceptable clothes for Adam and Eve? _____
   _____
   _____

5. When you were born, were you born into God's family or Adam's family? _____
   _____
   _____

6. Can you make yourself acceptable to God by doing good works? _____
   _____
   _____

7. Who is the only One who is acceptable and pleasing to God? _____
   _____

8. What did Jesus do for you so that you could be made acceptable to God? _____
   _____

9. If you have trusted in Jesus, does God see you as unacceptable? _____
   _____
   _____
   _____

10. Why did God make a way for you to be made acceptable to Him? _____
    _____
    _____
    _____

(Answers in *The Most Amazing Story*, page 515)

Lesson 72—**Eternal Life**

Memory Verse

> *For as in Adam all die, even so in Christ all shall be made alive. 1 Corinthians 15:22*

Questions

1. What happened to Adam and Eve's soul and spirit when they ate from The Tree of the Knowledge of Good and Evil?

   _____

   _____

   _____

2. What was going to happen to Adam and Eve when their bodies died?

   _____

   _____

3. When Cain and Abel were born, were they separated from God?

   _____

   _____

   _____

4. How did God show Cain and Abel that they could come to Him to be accepted?

   _____

   _____

   _____

5. Into whose family were you born?

   _____

6. When you were born, were you born separated from God?

   _____

   _____

7. What is the penalty for sin?

   _____

8. Who did God send to die in your place so that you do not have to die?

   _____

   _____

9. What do you need to do in order to receive eternal life?

   _____

   _____

   _____

   _____

(Answers in *The Most Amazing Story*, page 520)

Lesson 73—**Jesus is the Only Door**

Memory Verse

> *Salvation is found in no one else, for there is no other name under heaven given to men by which we must be saved. Acts 4:12*

Questions

1. How many doors were there into Noah's big boat? _____
   _____
   _____

2. How many entrances were there into a sheepfold? _____
   _____
   _____

3. How many ways are there for you to be saved from Satan and death? _____
   _____
   _____
   _____

4. Is there anything you can do to make yourself acceptable to God so that you can live with Him forever? _____
   _____
   _____
   _____

5. How is Jesus like the good shepherd? _____
   _____
   _____
   _____
   _____

6. What must you do to be able to go to Heaven? _____
   _____
   _____
   _____
   _____

(Answers in *The Most Amazing Story*, page 524)

Lesson 74—**Jesus Our Substitute**

Memory Verse

The next day John saw Jesus coming toward him, and said, "Behold! The Lamb of God who takes away the sin of the world!" John 1:29

Questions

1. What held Isaac on the altar so that he could not get off? _____
   _____
   _____

2. Who was the only One who could save Isaac from death?_____
   _____
   _____

3. What kind of substitute did God provide to die in Isaac's place?_____
   _____
   _____
   _____

4. In what way is your sin like the ropes that were tied around Isaac on the altar? _____
   _____
   _____
   _____

5. Can you free yourself from your sin? _____
   _____
   _____
   _____

6. Who is the only One who can provide a way for you to be saved from death? _____
   _____
   _____
   _____

7. Who did God provide to die in your place?_____
   _____
   _____
   _____

(Answers in *The Most Amazing Story*, page 530)

Lesson 76—**Friends, Not Enemies**

Memory Verse

But now in Christ Jesus you who once were far off have been brought near by the blood of Christ. Ephesians 2:13

Questions

1. Why can sinful people not live with God? _____
   _____

2. What was the only way for the Israelites to approach God? _____
   _____
   _____
   _____

3. How often did the Israelites have to sacrifice lambs? _____
   _____
   _____
   _____

4. Who did God choose to be the last High Priest? _____
   _____

5. How was Jesus' sacrifice better than the animal sacrifices? _____
   _____
   _____
   _____
   _____

6. Why did the curtain in the temple rip in two when Jesus died on the cross? _____
   _____
   _____
   _____

7. Why were you God's enemy? _____
   _____

8. What does it mean to be reconciled to God? _____
   _____

9. Who made it possible for us sinners to be made God's friends? _____
   _____

10. Since Jesus paid for everyone's sin, does that mean everyone will go to Heaven? ____
    _____
    _____

(Answers in *The Most Amazing Story*, page 542)

Lesson 76—The Last Passover Lamb

Memory Verse

> *For indeed Christ, our Passover, was sacrificed for us. 1 Corinthians 5:7b*

Questions

1. What was the last plague God sent on Egypt? _____
   _____
   _____

2. How could the firstborn sons of the Israelites be saved from death? _____
   _____
   _____
   _____
   _____

3. Why did God tell the Israelites to stay inside their homes after they sprinkled the
   blood on the doorframes? _____
   _____
   _____
   _____

4. Why were the Israelites not to break any of the bones of the lamb they killed? _____
   _____
   _____
   _____
   _____

5. Could the lambs chosen by the Israelites have any spots or blemishes? _____
   _____
   _____
   _____

6. Did Jesus ever sin? _____
   _____

7. What did John the Baptist call Jesus? _____
   _____

8. During what Jewish feast did Jesus die? _____
   _____

9. How is Jesus our a Passover Lamb? _____
   _____
   _____
   _____
   _____

(Answers in *The Most Amazing Story*, page 530)

Lesson 77—**Redeemed**

Memory Verse

[...] knowing that you were not redeemed with corruptible things, like silver or gold [...]
but with the precious blood of Christ, as of a lamb without blemish and without spot
1 Peter 1:18-19

Questions

1. Why do all people rightfully belong to God? _____
    _____
    _____

2. How did all the people in the world come to be under Satan's dominion? _____
    _____
    _____
    _____

3. What did God tell Satan would happen to his head in the Garden of Eden? _____
    _____
    _____
    _____
    _____

4. Who did God send to redeem you? _____
    _____

5. What is the payment for sin? _____
    _____

6. What is the payment Jesus paid for your sin? _____
    _____

7. What does the word gospel mean? _____
    _____

8. What is God's good news for you? _____
    _____
    _____
    _____

9. If you have trusted in Jesus as your Savior, who do you belong to? _____
    _____
    _____
    _____
    _____

(Answers in *The Most Amazing Story*, page 549)

Lesson 78—**Declared Righteous**

Memory Verse

[...] that we might be justified by faith in Christ and not by the works of the law; for by the works of the law no flesh shall be justified. Galatians 2:16b

Questions

1. How did the man who called Jesus Good Teacher think he could earn eternal life?
    _____
    _____

2. How good does a person have to be in order to live with God in Heaven?
    _____
    _____
    _____

3. Is there anyone who can be good enough to live with God?
    _____
    _____

4. What is the only way for you to get the righteousness you need to be able to live with God in Heaven?
    _____
    _____

5. When Jesus died on the cross, He took your sin on Himself so that He could give you His what? _____
    _____
    _____

6. Who is the Judge of all the earth?
    _____

7. What does the word justify mean?
    _____

8. How can God legally declare you righteous when you are a sinner?
    _____
    _____
    _____
    _____

9. How can you be declared righteous by God so that you can live with Him in Heaven?
    _____
    _____

(Answers in *The Most Amazing Story*, pages 554-555)

Lesson 79—**Safe and Secure**

Memory Verse

> *And I give them eternal life, and they shall never perish; neither shall anyone snatch them out of My hand. John 10:28*

Questions

1. Who comes to live inside of you when you trust Jesus as your Savior? _____
_____

2. Once you are born into God's family, can you become unborn? _____
_____
_____

3. Will God ever cast out any of His children? _____
_____

4. How long is eternal life? _____
_____
_____

5. If God gives you a gift, will He take it back? _____
_____
_____

6. If you have to work for or pay for something, is it a gift? _____
_____

7. Will God disown His children if they do not keep His rules? _____
_____
_____
_____
_____

8. As God's child, where does God hide you? _____

9. Could Satan and his demons, or anyone else, ever steal you away from God? _____
_____
_____

10. What two promises does God make to whoever believes in Jesus? _____
_____

11. Does God always keep His word? _____

12. Does God always finish what He starts? _____

13. What is the work God is doing in your life? _____
_____

14. Since you are God's child, where will you go when you die? _____
_____

(Answers in *The Most Amazing Story*, pages 561-562)

Lesson 80—**A New Identity**

Memory Verse

> *Therefore, if anyone is in Christ, he is a new creation; old things have passed away; behold, all things have become new. 2 Corinthians 5:17*

Questions

1. What was true of you in Adam? _____
   _____
   _____

2. What are some things that are true of you now that you are a new creation in Christ?
   _____
   _____
   _____
   _____
   _____

3. How does God communicate with you? _____
   _____

4. How can you communicate with God? _____
   _____
   _____

5. What does it mean to be dead to sin? _____
   _____

6. Now that you have trusted in Jesus Christ to save you, are you dead to God or alive to God? _____
   _____
   _____

7. Who lives inside of you to give you the strength to do what is right? _____
   _____
   _____

8. What does the word confess mean? _____
   _____

9. When you realize you have done something that displeases God, what does God want you to do? _____
   _____
   _____

10. Does God stop loving you when you do something that displeases Him? _____
    _____

(Answers in *The Most Amazing Story*, page 569)

Made in the USA
Columbia, SC
23 October 2020